Strong Defences

Guided/Group Reading Notes

Brown Band

Contents

OXFORD

Introduction

Reading progression in Year 3/Primary 4

By Year 3/P4 (ages 7–8), the majority of children have mastered the basics of learning to read. The focus is on continuing to build their engagement with reading, supporting reading confidence, further developing comprehension and increasing reading fluency. Phonic knowledge still plays a role in decoding some new words and in spelling but the majority of everyday words are now recognized automatically. Year 3/P4 children can read longer texts with less explicit support from repeated vocabulary and sentences and from pictures. Familiar and regular words, now part of children's sight vocabulary, are used to provide a secure reading base. New vocabulary is increasingly varied and includes polysyllabic and more complex topic-based words. Introducing new vocabulary within a meaningful context is an important element in extending children's vocabulary range.

The texts at **brown band** contain a variety of sentence structures, vocabulary and verb tenses. Children will encounter complex, fast-moving plots which engage interest and encourage the reader to read on through a whole book. The plot is developed over several chapters. Events are extended over a longer period of time. Some events may be told in a 'non-chronological' order through time-slip or flashback devices. Insights into characters' motives, feelings and actions become increasingly complex and characters are presented through a range of means: thoughts, feelings, behaviour, actions and responses to other characters. The consequences of actions are explored and moral dilemmas posed. Literary language is core and clearly distinct from the everyday language of character dialogue. Language play (puns, homonyms, jokes, onomatopoeia, etc.) can also be found in the texts. Stories are not merely straightforward recounts but demand inference, deduction and synthesizing of information from the reader.

In non-fiction books, the content of the text is largely outside of the reader's direct everyday experience – thus broadening their knowledge and their vocabulary. Texts have depth and lots of opportunity for the reader to infer, interpret and evaluate information – the text poses questions of the reader and/ or encourages them to want to investigate a subject further. The ratio of text to illustrations/photographs is greater, but the illustrations continue to provide additional information and interest for the reader, including opportunities to compare and contrast visual information and source materials.

A range of non-fiction features including charts, maps, tables, labelled diagrams, captions, index and glossaries are used to encourage children to read and interpret information presented in a variety of ways.

Visual literacy is supported through additional action and information in the illustrations, the use of graphic devices and cartoon and comic-strip genres and the suggestions for visualization comprehension strategies suggested in these notes.

Progression in the Project X character books

In this cluster, the children realize that they are about to be attacked by Dr X's miniature robots, the X-bots. They prepare their defences for the attack and then engage in a battle with the X-bots. They discover the capabilities (and limitations) of the X-bots and display their resourcefulness, bravery and loyalty. Readers will recognize that this attack is significant in that it shows how important recapturing the watches is to Dr X. They also learn more about Dr X's personality, his headquarters and about his two henchmen, Plug and Socket. The story ends on a cliff hanger so that readers are motivated to read on to the next level.

Guided/group reading

The engaging content and careful levelling of Project X books makes them ideal for use in guided/group reading sessions. The advantages of using guided/group reading, as well as charts to help you assess the appropriate level of reading group, are discussed in the *Teaching Handbook* for Year 3/P4.

To use the books in guided/group reading sessions, you should select a book at a band that creates a small degree of challenge for the group of pupils. Typically, children should be able to read about 90% of the book unaided. This level of 'readability' provides the context for children to practise their reading and build reading confidence. The 'challenge' in the text provides opportunities for explicitly teaching reading skills.

These *Guided/Group Reading Notes* provide support for each book in the cluster, along with suggestions for follow-up activities. Each book can be covered in up to three guided/group reading sessions.

Speaking, listening and drama

Talk is crucial to learning. Children need plenty of opportunities to express their ideas through talk and drama, and to listen to and watch the ideas of others. These processes are important for building reading engagement, personal response and understanding. Suggestions for speaking, listening and drama are given for every book.

Within these *Guided/Group Reading Notes* the speaking and listening activities are linked to the reading assessment focuses.

Building comprehension

Understanding what we have read is at the heart of reading. To help readers become effective in comprehending a text these *Guided/Group Reading Notes* contain practical strategies to develop the following important aspects of comprehension:

- Previewing
- Predicting
- Activating and building prior knowledge
- Questioning
- Recalling
- Visualizing and other sensory responses
- Deducting, inferring and drawing conclusions
- Determining importance
- Synthesizing
- Empathizing
- Summarizing
- Personal response, including adopting a critical stance

The research basis and rationale for focusing on these aspects of comprehension is given in the *Teaching Handbook* for Year 3/P4.

Reading fluency

Reading fluency combines automatic word recognition, reading with pace, and expression. Rereading, fluency and building comprehension are linked together in a complex interrelationship, where each supports the other. This is discussed more fully in the *Teaching Handbook* for Year 3/P4. Opportunities for children to read aloud are important in building fluency and reading aloud to children provides models of expressive fluent reading. Suggestions for purposeful and enjoyable oral reading and rereading/re-listening activities are given in the follow-up activities to guided/group reading and in the notes for parents on the inside cover of each book.

The Project X *Interactive Stories* software can be used to provide a model of reading fluency for the whole class and/or opportunities for individuals or small groups of children to listen to stories again and again. Listening to stories being read is particularly effective with EAL children.

Building vocabulary

Explicit work on enriching vocabulary is important in building reading fluency and comprehension. Repeatedly encountering a word and its variants helps it become known on sight. The thematic 'cluster' structure of Project X supports this because words are repeated within and across the books. Suggestions for vocabulary work are included in these notes. The vocabulary chart on pages 10 and 11 shows when vocabulary is repeated and new words are introduced. It also indicates those words that can be used to support learning alongside a structured phonics and spelling programme.

Developing a thematic approach

Helping children make links in their learning supports their development as learners. All the books in this cluster have a focus on the theme **Strong Defences**. A chart showing the cross-curricular potential of this theme is given in the *Teaching Handbook* for Year 3/P4, along with a rationale for using thematic approaches. Some suggestions for cross-curricular activities are also given in these notes, in the follow-up suggestions for each book.

In guided/group reading sessions, you will also want to encourage children to make links between the books in the cluster. Grouping books in a cluster allows readers to make links between characters, events and actions across the books. This enables readers to gradually build complex understandings of characters, to give reasons why things happen and how characters may change and develop. It can help them recognize cause and effect. It helps children reflect on the skill of determining importance, as a minor incident or detail in one book may prove to have greater significance when considered across several books.

Note that the 2-part Project X story should be read in order (*The X-Bots are Coming ...* before *Attack of the X-bots*), but all other books in the cluster can be read in any order.

In the **Strong Defences** cluster, some of the suggested links that can be explored include:

- designing a film poster for the film 'The X-bots are Coming...' (**Art and design**)
- producing an annotated drawing of X-bot Mark 3 (**DT**)
- experimenting to see why curved walls are stronger than walls with right angles (**Science**, **DT**)
- creating an electronic catalogue of protective clothing used in skateboarding, biking, fencing and motor racing. (**ICT**)

Reading into writing

The Project X books provide both models and inspiration to support children's writing. Brief suggestions for relevant, contextualized and interesting writing activities are given in the follow-up activities for each book. These include both short and longer writing opportunities. The activities cover a wide range of writing contexts so writers can develop an understanding of adapting their writing for different audiences and purposes.

The Project X *Interactive Stories* software contains a collection of 'clip art' assets from the characters books – characters, setting and props – that children can use in their writing.

Selecting follow-up activities

These *Guided/Group Reading Notes* give many ideas for follow-up activities. Some of these can be completed within the reading session. Some are longer activities that will need to be worked on over time. You should select those activities that are most appropriate for your pupils. It is not expected that you would complete all the suggested activities.

Home/school reading

Books used in a guided/group reading session can also be used in home/school reading programmes.

Before a guided/group reading session, the child could:

- read the first chapter/chapters and in the guided/group reading session begin at the next unread chapter
- read a related book from the cluster to build background knowledge.

Following a guided/group reading session, the child could:

- reread the book at home to build reading confidence and fluency
- read the next chapter in a longer book
- read a related book from the cluster.

Notes and guidance for parents on supporting their child in reading at home is provided in the inside covers of individual books. There is further advice for teachers concerning home/school reading partnerships in the *Teaching Handbook* for Year 3/P4.

Assessment

During guided/group reading, teachers make ongoing assessments of individuals and of the group. Reading targets are indicated for each book and you should assess against these. You should select just one or two targets at a time as the focus for the group. The same target can be appropriate for several literacy sessions or over several texts.

Readers should be encouraged to self-assess and peer-assess against the target/s.

Further support for assessing pupils' progress is provided in the *Teaching Handbook* for Year 3/P4.

Continuous reading objectives and ongoing assessment

The following objectives will continue to be consolidated in guided/ group reading sessions in Year 3/P4. Teachers will be aware of these objectives in their ongoing assessment but will only specifically assess against these objectives for children who are not making the expected rate of progress:

- Read independently and with increasing fluency longer and less familiar texts **5.1**
- Know how to tackle unfamiliar words that are not completely decodable **5.3**
- Read and spell less common alternative graphemes including trigraphs **5.4**
- Read high and medium frequency words independently and automatically **5.5**

The following objective will be supported in every guided/group reading session and is therefore a *continuous* focus for attention and assessment (AF1). This objective is not repeated in full in each set of notes but as you listen to individual children reading you should undertake ongoing assessment, against this objective:

- Use syntax and context to build their store of vocabulary when reading for meaning **7.4**

Further framework objectives are provided as a focus within the notes for each book. Correlation to the specific objectives/guidelines within the Scottish, Welsh and Northern Ireland curricula are provided in the *Teaching Handbook* for Year 3/P4.

 ## Recording assessment

The assessment chart for the **Strong Defences** cluster is provided in the *Teaching Handbook* for Year 3/P4.

 ## Diagnostic assessment

If an individual child is failing to make good progress or he or she seems to have a specific problem with some aspect of reading you will want to undertake a more detailed assessment. Details of how to use running records for diagnostic assessment are given in the *Teaching Handbook* for Year 3/P4.

Vocabulary chart

At Year 3/P4, the children should:

- read high and medium frequency words independently and automatically
- read and spell
  - compound words and polysyllabic words
  - prefixes and suffixes
  - unfamiliar words using known conventions.

NB Examples only are given in each category.

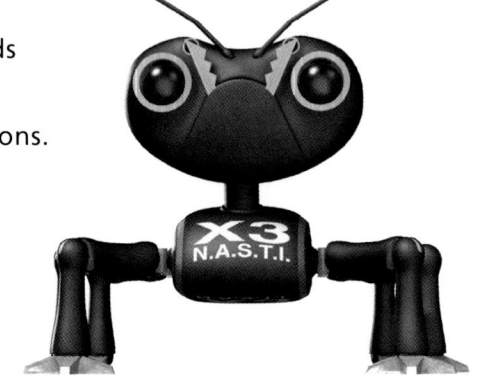

The X-bots are Coming ...	Phonetically regular compound and polysyllabic words	temporary, production, assigned, certificate, dangerous, remote-controlled, calculations, microphone
	Prefixes/suffixes	**-ly** secretly, brightly, firmly, gingerly, quickly, finally, rapidly, exactly, actually, proudly, surely, definitely, urgently
	Context vocabulary	army, captured, castle, moat, defences, catapult, camouflaged, defend, attack
Attack of the X-bots!	Phonetically regular compound and polysyllabic words	propeller, amphibious, scientific, experiments, microphone, helicopter, tantrum, direction, triumphantly, abandoned
	Prefixes/suffixes	**-er** stronger, meaner, faster, lower **-est** bravest, cleverest
	Context vocabulary	army, fight, escape, defences, scared, marched, conquer, catapult, castle, destroyed, retreat, trap, march, drawbridge, tower, circuits, magnet, magnetism

Under Attack!	**Phonetically regular compound and polysyllabic words**	enormous, lanterns, important, projected, sometimes
	Prefixes/suffixes **Using core word for spelling**	**under-** underneath, underground **-tion** protection, ammunition, bastions Word families 'defend' and 'invade'
	Context vocabulary	security, alarm, invaders, drawbridge, fortified, enemy, soldiers, ramparts, siege, keep, trebuchet, mangonel, archer, notorious
Lone Wolf	**Phonetically regular compound and polysyllabic words**	murmured, bullet, yelping, burrowed, grandma, important, whimpering, fuzzballs, crunch, territory, whirlpools, thunder, loneliness, sideways, quivered, joyful, leadership
	Prefixes/suffixes	**re-** reunion, return **-ly** carefully, prickly, eagerly, pitifully, mournfully, suddenly, instantly, joyfully, finally, excitedly, noisily, desperately, proudly, furiously, silently, friendly
	Context vocabulary	snarls, howls, pounce, hunting, loping, she-wolf, fangs, hooves, antlers, marrow, coat, pack, wilderness, carcass
Strong Defences	**Phonetically regular compound and polysyllabic words**	security, devices, virus, invaders, sneezes, harmless, smallpox, hummingbird, temperature, underground, lookout, elephant, parasites, relationship, meteorite, communication
	Prefixes/suffixes	**un-** unwell, unfriendly **-ious** infectious **-iable** sociable
	Context vocabulary	viruses, antibodies, immunity, vaccines, bacteria, blood, polio, vaccinated, measles, mumps, parasites, territory, Bangladesh, Martians, extraterrestrials, satellites

The X-bots are Coming ...

BY ANTHONY McGOWAN

About this book

As Dr X has discovered the micro-friends' hideout in the old tree stump, the children move to Tiger's castle on the island of the park pond. They set up various traps to defend themselves against attack from the X-bots.

You will need

- *Den locations* Photocopy Master, *Teaching Handbook* for Year 3/P4
- *Character profile* Photocopy Master, *Teaching Handbook* for Year 3/P4
- *Castle for sale* Photocopy Master *Teaching Handbook* for Year 3/P4

	Literacy Framework objective	Target and assessment focus
Speaking, listening, group interaction and drama	○ Use some drama strategies to explore stories or issues **4.2**	○ We can freeze frame to explore our understanding of stories **AF2/3**
Reading See also continuous reading objectives listed on page 9.	○ Empathize with characters **8.2** ○ Identify features that writers use to provoke readers' reactions **8.3**	○ We can empathize with characters' feelings and actions **AF3** ○ We can discuss how authors create effects, including their choice of vocabulary **AF2/5**

The following notes provide a structure for three guided/group reading sessions. They are intended to be used flexibly; you may choose to focus on all three sessions or you could focus on one session and have the children read the rest of the book independently. In Session 1, children will read Chapters 1–3. In Session 2, they will read Chapters 4–6. In Session 3, children will read Chapters 7–9.

Session I (Chapters I–3)

 Before reading

To activate prior knowledge and encourage prediction

- Look at the cover and ask children to recall the X-bots in other stories. Do they notice anything new or different about the X-bot on the front cover? (**activating prior knowledge**)
- Show the cover of the second book (*Attack of the X-bots!*) and ask them how they think the two books might link together. (**predicting**)

To support decoding, word recognition and introduce new vocabulary

- Help the children decode some of the context vocabulary related to attacking and defending and use syntax and context to work out their meaning, e.g. *moat* (p.18), *defences* (p.34), *attack* (p.35), *capture* (p.37). Start creating a list of words for a word wall.

During reading

- Ask the children to read, from the beginning of the book to the end of Chapter 3.
- As they read, ask them to think about how the author shows the different emotions the friends are feeling. Ask them to jot down any vocabulary related to how they feel or act.
- If you have not already done so, ask the children what to do if they encounter a difficult word, modelling with an example from the book if necessary.

> **Assessment point**
>
> Listen to individual children reading and make ongoing assessments on their decoding, sight vocabulary, approaches to tackling new words and their reading fluency. **AF1**

After reading

Returning to the text

- Ask the children to describe the friends' different reactions to the need to move their secret base. What vocabulary helps us to understand these reactions? (**recall**)

- Can the children explain why Dr X was giving Plug and Socket new roles? How did Plug and Socket feel about this? (**deducing, inferring, drawing conclusions**)

- Ask the children to identify the weakness in the plan to put the den up the tree. How did Max show leadership skills? (**determining importance**)

- Why did Max ask if everyone could swim *before* he suggested the island? What does that tell you about Max? (**deducing, inferring**)

Building comprehension

- Ask the children to use the *Character profiles* Photocopy Master for any/all of the characters if they think they have identified new information about that character. Remind them that they must be able to quote evidence from the text. (**deducing, inferring, synthesizing**)

· ·>

- Ask the children to list the pros and cons for each of the secret bases, using the *Den locations* Photocopy Master. (**deducing, inferring, drawing conclusions**)

Session 2 (Chapters 4–6)

 Before reading

To activate prior knowledge and encourage prediction

- Ask the children to recap on the story so far. What do they think will happen in the middle of the story? (**activating prior knowledge, predicting**)

To support decoding, word recognition and introduce new vocabulary

- Point out the unusual spelling of the plural word *larvae* (p.23) and ask the children to guess what the singular form is. Discuss other similar words that the children might know, e.g. 'antenna/antennae'.
- You may also wish to point out some of the high or medium frequency words or practise decoding some of the phonically regular words in this book and listed in the vocabulary chart on page 10.

 During reading

- Ask the children to read Chapters 4–6.
- As they read, ask them to think about how the characters, including Dr X, Plug and Socket, are thinking and feeling.

 After reading

Returning to the text

- Ask the children:
  - Why was the island a good base?
  - What do we learn about Tiger's character from his actions in Chapter 4?
  - How does the author build tension at the end of Chapter 6? (**deducing, inferring, drawing conclusions**)

Building comprehension

- Ask the children to freeze frame the moment on page 30 when Dr X discovers the children have moved their base.

· >

Assessment point

Can the children freeze frame to explore their understanding of the story? **AF2/3**

15

Session 3 (Chapters 7-9)

 Before reading

To activate prior knowledge and encourage prediction

- Ask the children to recap on the story so far. Reminding them that there is a sequel story (*Attack of the X-bots!*), how do they think this story will end? (**activating prior knowledge, predicting**)

To support decoding, word recognition and introduce new vocabulary

- Explain how children can use the description in the text and the picture to clarify the meaning of the word *catapult* on page 38.

 During reading

- Ask the children to read Chapters 7-9.
- As they read, ask them to think about how the author creates tension in these chapters.

 After reading

Returning to the text

- Ask the children to briefly describe the different traps that the micro-friends devise. (**recall**)
- Ask why the micro-friends are feeling happy at the start of Chapter 9, then track how their emotions change during the chapter. (Firstly, they feel happy, become concerned, triumphant, very afraid, then finally, feel brave). Can the children spot the vocabulary, speech and actions that help them to identify these changing emotions? Which emotions do they infer? (e.g. The friend's triumph when they hit an X-bot.) (**deducing, inferring, drawing conclusions**)
- Ask the children to identify the cliff-hanger at the end of the story. How does this create tension? How does it make the reader feel? (**personal response**)

· ·>

> **Assessment point**
>
> Can the children identify how the author creates effects such as tension and the impact this has on readers? Can they recognize how the author's choice of vocabulary achieves this? AF2/5

Building fluency

- Invite the children to enact some of the scenes at the NASTI headquarters, in particular Dr X's speech to the robots. Then ask them to reread these chapters aloud using as much expression as possible.

Follow-up activities

Writing activities

- Write an estate agent's blurb for the castle on the island, using the *Castle for sale* Photocopy Master. (**short writing task**)
- Write a longer speech for Dr X to deliver to the X-bots in which he tells them more about why he needs the watches, as well as praising their design, intelligence, strength, etc. (**longer writing task**)

Other possible literacy activities

- Children could perform or record for other members of the group their Dr X speech (see Writing activities).
- Collect words with the suffix –ly in the story. Can the children generate a spelling rule for adding –ly to words?

Cross-curricular and thematic opportunities

- Produce a design brief for the X-bot Mark 3. (**DT**)
- Use Ant's description of pond life as the stimulus for further research on one of the creatures and their defence/attack mechanisms. (**Science**)
- Use musical instruments to create marching music for the 'March of the X-bots'. (**Music**)
- Design a film poster for the film 'The X-bots are Coming'. (**Art and design**)

Attack of the X-bots!

BY ANTHONY McGOWAN

About this book

This sequel to *The X-bots are Coming ...* describes how the micro-friends defend their castle from the X-bots' attack, using various strategies and traps: creating a diversion to lead them towards the pike; short-circuiting them by catapulting water balloons; trapping them with sticky bubblegum; disrupting their circuits using the magnet. Finally, Cat uses bread to entice the ducks to trample the X-bots!

You will need

- *Character profile* Photocopy Master, *Teaching Handbook* for Year 3/P4

- *Problems and outcomes* Photocopy Master, *Teaching Handbook* for Year 3/P4

	Literacy Framework objective	Target and assessment focus
Speaking, listening, group interaction and drama	○ Explain process or present information ensuring that items are clearly sequenced, relevant details are included and accounts are ended effectively **1.2**	○ We can present a detailed account of an episode in the story, giving the events in the correct order **AF2**
Reading See also continuous reading objectives listed on page 9.	○ Infer characters' feelings in fiction **7.2** ○ Empathise with characters **8.2** ○ Identify features that writers use to provoke readers' reations **8.3**	○ We can work out how characters feel from their words and actions **AF3** ○ We can discuss how authors create effects, including their choice of vocabulary **AF2/5**

The following notes provide a structure for three guided/group reading sessions. They are intended to be used flexibly; you may choose to focus on all three sessions or you could focus on one session and have the children read the rest of the book independently. In Session 1, children will read Chapters 1–4. In Session 2, they will read Chapters 5 and 6. In Session 3, children will read Chapters 7–9.

Session I (Chapters I–4)

 Before reading

To activate prior knowledge and encourage prediction

- Read pages 2 and 3 together and recap the details of the traps the micro-friends have prepared for the X-bots.
- Discuss what else will offer the children protection from attack (e.g. water, walls). (**activating prior knowledge**, **predicting**)

To support decoding and word recognition and introduce new vocabulary

- Help the children decode some of the context vocabulary related to attacking and defending and use syntax and context to work out their meaning, e.g. *diversion* (p.11), *conquer* (p.13). Start or continue creating a list of words for a word wall.

 During reading

- Ask the children to read Chapters 1–4.
- As they read, ask them to think about the changing emotions the friends and Dr X are feeling as the attack occurs.
- If you have not already done so, ask the children what to do if they encounter a difficult word, modelling with an example from the book if necessary. Remind them of the more challenging vocabulary which you looked at before reading the book.

> **Assessment point**
>
> Listen to individual children reading and make ongoing assessments on their decoding, sight vocabulary, approaches to tackling new words and their reading fluency. AF1

After reading

Returning to the text

- Ask the children why the friends decided they must fight the X-bots.

- Ask the children to describe, in sequence, the first two attacks from the X-bots by water and by air, and the defences that were used by the friends. (**recall**)

· ·>

Building comprehension

- Talk about the different responses of each character to the X-bots' first transformation (pages 8–9). Does this add to or confirm what they already know about each child's character? Children could add to the *Character profile* Photocopy Masters for any/all of the characters. (**deducing, inferring, drawing conclusions**)

- Complete the *Problems and outcomes* Photocopy Master to show how the problems encountered in the book were overcome by the children. This can be continued after each session and will provide a prompt sheet or talking frame for children to give a sequenced, oral account of the story. (**determining importance**)

Building vocabulary

- Look for words that use the suffix 'er', e.g. *meaner* (p.7), *faster* (p.14). Discuss their superlative form.

Session 2 (Chapters 5 and 6)

 Before reading

To activate prior knowledge and encourage prediction

- Recap the story so far. Encourage the children to predict what will happen next, reminding them of the traps that the friends developed beforehand. (**activating prior knowledge, predicting**)

To support decoding and word recognition and introduce new vocabulary

- Continue or start to create a word wall relating to defending and attacking using words from these chapters.

 During reading

- Ask the children to read Chapters 5 and 6.
- As they read, ask them to think about the author's choice of vocabulary to show the humour in Plug and Socket.

 After reading

Returning to the text

Ask the children:

- Why is the X-bot called 'the X-bot mole' on page 25?
- What is it that Ant notices when Max first uses the magnet on the X-bot? (p.32) Why is this important later in the chapter?
- What do Max's actions in Chapter 6 tell us about his character? What evidence can you find to back up your views?
- As well as 'nincompoops' (p.29), what words and actions are used to show that Plug and Socket are not very clever? (**deducing, inferring, drawing conclusions**)

> **Assessment point**
>
> Do the children understand how the author's vocabulary choice affects the reader's response to the characters? **AF2/AF5**

···➤

Building comprehension

- Start or continue to fill in the *Problems and outcomes* Photocopy Master to show how the problems encountered in the book were overcome by the friends. (**determining importance**)

Session 3 (Chapters 7-9)

 Before reading

To activate prior knowledge and encourage prediction

● Ask the children, in turn, to relay the events of the story so far. (**activating prior knowledge**)

● Read page 38 together. Can the children guess where Cat is going and why? (**predicting**)

To support decoding and word recognition and introduce new vocabulary

● Continue or start to create a word wall relating to defending and attacking using words from these chapters, e.g. *drawbridge* (p.39), *trampled* (p.44), *retreat* (p.45).

 During reading

● Ask the children to read Chapters 7-9.

● As they read, ask them to think about how the characters' words and actions reveal their personalities.

 After reading

Returning to the text

● Ask the children:
  ○ What do Ant and Tiger think Cat is doing when she leaves the castle? Do you agree or disagree with the way they reacted to her leaving? What are your reasons/evidence?
  ○ Why does Max jump down from his safe refuge in the tree? What does this tell you about Max's character?
  ○ Do Dr X and Plug and Socket have the same feelings about the failed attack?
  ○ Why do they think the author ends the story with the final sentence? (**deducing, inferring, drawing conclusions**)

Building comprehension

- Ask the children to continue (or start) filling in their *Character profile* Photocopy Master, adding evidence that shows each character's personality. (**deducing, inferring, drawing conclusions**)

··>

- Ask the children to complete their *Problems and outcomes* Photocopy Master to use later as a prompt sheet for their oral re-telling of the story (see Other literacy activities). (**determining importance**)

<table>
<tr><td>**Assessment point**</td></tr>
<tr><td>Can the children deduce how characters feel from their words and actions? AF3</td></tr>
</table>

Follow-up activities

Writing activities

- Write an advertisement or sales blurb for the X-bot Mark 3. (**short writing task**)
- Write a newspaper report of the battle with a suitable headline. (**longer writing task**)
- Turn the scenes in NASTI headquarters into a play script. (**longer writing task**)

Other literacy activities

- Invite the children to give an oral re-telling of the story. (**speaking and listening**)
- Look at the simile used to describe the flying X-bots on page 14. Ask the children to create similes for the clicking jaws (p.18), Dr X stomping up and down (p.22), the drumming feet (p.25), the loud clanging noise (p.30) and the enormous size of the ducks (p.41).

Cross-curricular and thematic opportunities

- Annotate the X-bot design sheet started in *The X-bots are Coming ...* with the new features now revealed. (**DT**)
- Experiment with magnets and a selection of materials to discover which are magnetic and which cannot be magnetized. (**Science**)
- Use musical instruments to create background music for one of the chapters in the book. (**Music**)
- Devise an 'X-bot attack' board game which involves throwing dice and counting round a board. (**Maths, DT**)

Under Attack!

BY MICK GOWAR

About this book

This non-fiction text explains different methods used for defence: water, walls, weapons, alarms and security cameras. It also features impressive examples of defences from around the world, such as famous castles and walls.

You will need

- *Note-taking frame* Photocopy Master, *Teaching Handbook* for Year 3/P4

	Literacy Framework objective	**Target and assessment focus**
Speaking, listening, group interaction and drama	○ Develop and use specific vocabulary in different contexts 1.4 ○ Follow up others' points and show whether they agree or disagree 2.1	○ We can debate issues using evidence from the text, listening carefully and responding to other people's points **AF2/3**
Reading See also continuous reading objectives listed on page 9.	○ Identify and make notes of the main points of sections of texts 7.1 ○ Use syntax, context and word structure to build their store of vocabulary as they read for meaning 7.4	○ We can make notes of the main points of sections of a text **AF2** ○ We can use the context to work out the meaning of unfamiliar words **AF1**

The following notes provide a structure for three guided/group reading sessions. They are intended to be used flexibly; you may choose to focus on all three sessions or you could focus on one session and have the children read the rest of the book independently. In Session 1, children will read up to page 9. In Session 2, they will read pages 10–15. Children will then need to read pages 16–21 independently, prior to Session 3. In Session 3, children will read pages 22–30.

Session 1 (pages 2–9)

Before reading

To activate prior knowledge and encourage prediction

- Look at the front cover and title. Ask the children how they think this book will fit into the theme of strong defences. (**predicting**)

- Ask them to recall any castles they have visited or seen on film. What defensive features did they have? (**activating prior knowledge**)

To preview the text

- Look at the contents page. Ask the children to identify the five different categories of defensive features the book describes. Categorize them into ones which were used hundreds of years ago and ones which are more modern.

During reading

- Ask the children to read to the end of page 9.
- As they read ask them to notice the different ways water is used as a defensive feature.
- If you have not already done so, ask the children what to do if they encounter a difficult word, modelling with an example from the book if necessary.

· →

Assessment point

Listen to individual children reading and make ongoing assessments on their decoding, sight vocabulary, approaches to tackling new words and their reading fluency. **AF1**

After reading

Returning to the text

- Ask the children to:
  - give some reasons why water is a good form of defence
  - explain how people got across the moats
  - give some examples of castles where the sea was used as a defence. (**recall**)

Building comprehension

- Ask the children to use the photograph on page 8 to draw a bird's eye view of the castle and its moat. (**visualizing**)
- Allow children time to make notes on the *Note-taking frame* Photocopy Master on the pages read during this session. (**determining importance**, **summarizing**)

· >

> **Assessment point**
>
> Can children make notes of the main points of the pages they have read? AF2

Building vocabulary

- Record words that relate to attacking, defending, people who live or work in castles, and weapons.

Session 2 (pages 10–15)

 Before reading

- Ask the children to recap what they learnt about water defences. (**recall**, **summarizing**)

To preview the text

- Look at the next heading in the contents page: 'Walls'. Can the children predict how walls could be a good form of defence? (**predicting**, **deducing**, **inferring**, **drawing conclusions**)

To support decoding and word recognition and introduce new vocabulary

- You may wish to point out some of the high or medium frequency words or practise decoding some of the phonically regular words in this book and listed in the vocabulary chart on page 11.

During reading

- Ask the children to read pages 10–15.
- As they read, ask them to notice the different types of walls used for defence.

 After reading

Returning to the text

- Ask the children to:
  - give reasons why walls are a good form of defence
  - give some examples of castles built on cliffs or hills. Why are these difficult to attack? Encourage them to draw information from the illustrations as well as the text.
  - Why do they think sloping walls were used for some castles? (**recall**, **deducing**, **inferring**, **drawing conclusions**)

Building comprehension

- Allow children time to make notes on the *Note-taking frame* Photocopy Master on the pages read during this session. (**determining importance**, **summarizing**)

· ·➔

- Before Session 3, ask the children to read pages 16–21 independently.

> **Assessment point**
>
> Can the children continue to make notes of the main points of the pages they have read? Pairs of children could swap notes. Ask each child to comment on their partner's notes. Have they included all of the main points? (Peer assessment) AF2

Session 3 (pages 22–30)

 Before reading

- Ask the children to recap what kind of ammunition and defences were used during a siege or attack. (**recall**, **summarizing**)
- Invite the children to explain why an arrow slit was used by an archer, synthesizing the information from both the text and illustrations on pages 10 and 20. (**synthesizing**)

*To support decoding and word recognition and introduce
new vocabulary*

- Check the children's understanding and pronunciation of the names of the weapons – *trebuchet* (p.18) and *mangonel* (p.19) and other defence/attack words such as *ammunition* (p.18).

- Ask the children to explain how they worked out the meanings of these words by using the context.

> **Assessment point**
>
> Can the children say how the context helped them to work out the meaning of these unfamiliar words? **AF1**

• >

 During reading

- Ask the children to read pages 22–30.
- As they read, ask them to decide whether they are for or against security cameras based on the discussion points outlined in the text.

 After reading

Returning to the text

- Ask the children why alarms protect people. Why are closed circuit alarms placed by doors and windows? Why do alarms often make a lot of noise? (**recall**, **deducing**, **inferring**, **drawing conclusions**)

Building comprehension

- Allocate to each child one reason for or against security cameras. Ask them to come up with an example or evidence to support their point. Hold a class debate on the issue. (**synthesizing**)

> **Assessment point**
>
> Do the children use relevant information to support their point of view? Do the other children respond appropriately to each view? **AF2/3**

• >

- Allow children time to make notes on the *Note-taking frame* Photocopy Master on the pages read during this session. (**determining importance**, **summarizing**)

Building vocabulary

- Create word families for the core words *invade* (*invaders, invasive, invasion, invading*) and *defend* (*defenders, defensive, defences, defending*), noticing how the changes are made to the core word to create new words.

Follow-up activities

Writing activities

- Reread the nursery rhyme 'Humpty Dumpty' on page 21. Consider its rhythm and simple rhyme structure. Write a rhyme about one of the attacks by the X-bots. Children could use one of these starting lines or invent their own:
  - Twenty X-bots crossing a pond ...
  - A fleet of X-bots high in the sky ... (**short writing task**)
- Design warning signs for guard dogs and other animal guards. (**short writing task**)
- Write an imaginary account of a siege using siege weaponry and machinery from the point of view of an attacker or a defender. (**longer writing task**)

Other literacy activities

- Using the notes made on the *Note-taking frame* Photocopy Master, ask children to prepare a brief talk on strong defences. They could make an audio recording of the report. (**speaking and listening**)

Cross-curricular and thematic opportunities

- Visit a local castle and look at its defensive features. (**History**)
- Build a model castle with several defensive features. (**DT**)
- Experiment to see why curved walls are stronger than walls with right angles. (**Science**, **DT**)
- Make a simple buzzer alarm based on an electric circuit. (**Science**)
- Make a freeze frame animation of a castle attack using the model castle and small world figures. Record a sound track for the film. (**ICT**, **Music**)
- Play a game of football, netball or another attacking/defending game. Video the game. Watch it to identify and analyze points where the defence was particularly strong or particularly weak and identify why. (**PE**)

Lone Wolf

BY SUSAN GATES

About this book

This story tracks the life of Grey – a wolf cub who is shot and separated from his family pack. Through his difficulties he develops independence and determination that makes him a great leader to a large pack of wolves.

You will need

- *Wolf words* Photocopy Master, *Teaching Handbook* for Year 3/P4
- *Timeline of Grey's awful day* Photocopy Master, *Teaching Handbook* for Year 3/P4

	Literacy Framework objective	Target and assessment focus
Speaking, listening, group interaction and drama	○ Use the language of possibility to investigate and reflect on feelings, behaviour or relationships 3.3	○ We can discuss the story and reflect on it AF2/3
Reading See also continuous reading objectives listed on page 9.	○ Infer characters' feelings 7.2 ○ Empathize with characters 8.2 ○ Explore how different texts appeal to readers using varied sentence structures and descriptive language 7.5	○ We can work out how characters feel from their actions and empathize with them AF2/3 ○ We can identify descriptive language and discuss how it appeals to us AF5

The following notes provide a structure for three guided/group reading sessions. They are intended to be used flexibly; you may choose to focus on all three sessions or you could focus on one session and have the children read the rest of the book independently. In Session 1, children will read Chapters 1–3. In Session 2, they will read Chapters 4 and 5. In Session 3, children will Chapters 6–8.

Session 1 (Chapters 1–3)

 Before reading

To activate prior knowledge and encourage prediction

- Ask the children what stories they know about wolves, e.g. 'Little Red Riding Hood'. What characteristics does the wolf have in these stories? What facts – if any – do the children know about wolves? (**activating prior knowledge**)
- Do they see any contradiction in the title *Lone Wolf?* What does the title make them think the story might be about? (**predicting**)

To preview the text

- Read the back cover blurb and read the chapter titles. What does the final heading 'Grey's pack' suggest about the ending? (**previewing, predicting**)

To engage readers and encourage fluent reading

- Read the opening page aloud to the group. Then ask them in pairs to read it to each other, using expression. Ask them not to read on to the next page, until told to do so.

 During reading

- Ask the children to reread the opening page again, silently, and then read on to the end of Chapter 3.
- As they read, ask them to notice who is in the wolf pack and what are their different roles.

- If you have not already done so, ask the children what to do if they encounter a difficult word, modelling with an example from the book if necessary.

• •➤

After reading

Returning to the text

- Ask the children:
  - Why has the author started with the shooting incident?
  - How does she make us feel sorry for the cub? (By the descriptions and words suggesting Grey's vulnerability.)

• •➤

- In what ways does the wolf pack defend their cubs?
- What features of the wolves physical characteristics help it to defend itself?
- How did Grey get separated from his family? Was it his own fault? (**deducing, inferring, drawing conclusions**)

Building comprehension

- Begin filling in the *Timeline of Grey's awful day* Photocopy Master. (**summarizing**)
- Ask the children to describe how Grey must feel being away from his family. How do they think his close family members, especially Grandma, must be feeling? (**empathizing**)

• •➤

Building fluency

- Record the chapter describing Grey's adventure in the river. Add the sound effects of water and wolves howling. (**visualizing and other sensory responses**)

Session 2 (Chapters 4 and 5)

 Before reading

To activate prior knowledge and encourage prediction

- Ask the children to recap what has happened in the story so far. **(activating prior knowledge)**
- Can they deduce by the headings what the next two chapters will be about? **(predicting, deducing, inferring, drawing conclusions)**

To support decoding and word recognition and introduce new vocabulary

- You may wish to point out some of the high or medium frequency words or practise decoding some of the phonically regular words in this book and listed in the vocabulary chart on page 11.

 During reading

- Ask the children to read Chapters 4 and 5.
- As they read, ask them to think about what things go well and what things go badly for Grey.

 After reading

Returning to the text

- Ask the children:
  - How did the family try to get Grey back?
  - Why did Grey's mum keep howling?
  - What things went badly and what things went well for Grey in these chapters?
  - Do they think Grey will survive? **(deducing, inferring, drawing conclusions)**

Building comprehension

- Ask the children to describe some of the incidents in these two chapters from Grey's viewpoint. **(empathizing, deducing, inferring, drawing conclusions)**

> **Assessment point**
>
> Can the children articulate how the character feels, describing words and actions he might use?
> AF2/3

33

Session 3 (Chapters 6–8)

 Before reading

To activate prior knowledge and encourage prediction
- Ask the children to recap what has happened in the story so far. (**activating prior knowledge**)
- Look at the last three chapter headings. How do they think Grey's life is turning around? (**predicting, deducing, inferring, drawing conclusions**)

 During reading

- Ask the children to read Chapters 6–8.
- As they read, ask them to notice how the author portrays Grey in these chapters.

 After reading

Returning to the text
- Ask the children:
  - Why does Grey quiver with excitement on page 36?
  - Why did Grey and the other wolf fight when Grey approached the pack?
  - Why do you think the attacking pack spread out when they were about to attack Grey's pack?
  - How did the wolves recognize each other as family? (By sound and smell.)
  - What image of Grey is created in Chapter 8? How does the author do this?

Building comprehension
- Create a timeline for Grey's life, outlining Grey's life from birth to becoming the leader of the large pack.

Building vocabulary

- Search for and list all the words that describe the settings. What impression of the countryside do these give?

- List words to describe the noises Grey makes. Sort these into categories, e.g. noises when he is feeling frightened or alone; noises when he is feeling at ease/in a pack. What effect do these words have on the reader?

> **Assessment point**
>
> Can the children identify descriptive language and discuss how it appeals to the reader? AF5

Follow-up activities

Writing activities

- Discuss the children's overall impressions of the book. Invite them to write a book review for this story. (**longer writing task**)

- Make a comic strip or graphic novel version of the incident with the hunter or another dramatic incident in the story, using speech and thought bubbles and captions to tell the story. (**short writing task**)

- Using the book and other sources, write a non-information report on wild wolves and their lives. (**longer writing task**)

Other literacy activities

- Ask the children to imagine they are a hunter and to justify to a partner their decision to shoot a young wolf. (**speaking and listening**)

- List words describing a wolf's physical appearance. Write these around the picture on the *Wolf words* Photocopy Master.

Cross-curricular and thematic opportunities

- Research and map places where wolves still live in the wild. (**Geography**)

- Turn the information report on wolves into a software presentation and encourage the children to deliver this to other classes. (**ICT**)

- Consider the arguments for and against hunting. (**PSHE**)

- Listen to a recording of *Peter and the Wolf* and/or watch a film of the story. (**Music**)

Strong Defences

BY HAYDN MIDDLETON

About this book

This non-fiction book uses both formal and informal report styles to explore strong defences adopted by humans and animals.

You will need

• *Word detectives* Photocopy Master, *Teaching Handbook* for Year 3/P4

	Literacy Framework objective	Target and assessment focus
Speaking, listening, group interaction and drama	○ Identify the presentational features used to communicate the main points in a broadcast **2.2**	○ We can listen to and create a radio broadcast using appropriate presentational features **AF2**
Reading See also continuous reading objectives listed on page 9.	○ Identify how different texts are organized **7.3** ○ Share and compare reasons for reading preferences **8.1**	○ We can distinguish between the different kinds of texts in a book and say how they are organised **AF4** ○ We can say which book we prefer and why **AF4/5**

The following notes provide a structure for three guided/group reading sessions. They are intended to be used flexibly. In Session 1, children will read up to page 9. In Session 2, they will read pages 10–19. In Session 3, they will read pages 20–30.

Session 1 (pages 2–9)

 Before reading

To activate prior knowledge and encourage prediction

- Ask the children what they know about how animals and humans defend themselves.

To preview the text

- Read page 2 together. Discuss whether the bullet point list outlines the structure and content of the book. Compare this list to the contents page. Do they cover the same topics? Why has author has structured this page in this way? (**previewing**)

To engage readers and encourage fluent reading

- Ask someone in the group to read the page written by the doctor (p.3). Then ask the children to explain what they think the three ways mean before telling them to read on independently.

 During reading

- Ask the children to read to the end of page 9.
- As they read, ask them to look out for scientific words such as *virus*, *vaccination*, *temperature* and *energy*.
- If you have not already done so, ask the children what to do if they encounter a difficult word, modelling with an example from the book if necessary.

• •➤

Assessment point

Listen to individual children reading and make ongoing assessments on their decoding, sight vocabulary, approaches to tackling new words and their reading fluency. AF1.

After reading

Returning to the text
- Ask the children:
  - What are the three ways your body can fight viruses?
  - What can combat bacteria?
- Can they give two examples of how plants and animals save energy?

Building comprehension
- Ask the children to summarize the information on these pages into three or four main points for each topic covered. (**summarizing, determining importance**)
- Encourage the children to debate the claim 'attack is the best form of defence'. (**adopting a critical stance**)

Building vocabulary
- Create lists of scientific words as the children read, using the *Word detectives* Photocopy Master.

Session 2 (pages 10–19)

 Before reading

To activate prior knowledge and encourage prediction
- Ask the children to describe as many examples of defence that they have read about so far. Compare these with the features listed in Session 1. (**activating prior knowledge**)

To preview the text
- Glance through pages 10–19. What topics are being discussed? (**previewing**)

 During reading

- Ask the children to read pages 10–19.
- As they read, ask them to look at the ways the information is presented.

After reading

Returning to the text

- Ask the children:
  - How is the Martian report on pages 10–13 organized? (Chronologically, gives a description with an example.)
  - What are the organizational and language features of the catalogue? (pp.14–15)
  - How does the naturalist's report (pp.16–19) differ from the formal Martian's report?

Assessment point

Can the children distinguish between the different kinds of texts in the book and say how they are organized? **AF4**

Building comprehension

- Create a grid comparing the defensive features of castles and gated communities. Additional information can be taken from *Under Attack!* (**synthesizing**)

To engage readers and encourage fluent reading

- Allow the children, in pairs, to read the advertisements of defensive devices (pp.14–15) to each other in the style of television advertising.

Session 3 (pages 20–30)

 Before reading

To activate prior knowledge and encourage prediction

- Ask the children to summarize the defences they have read so far that animals use. (**activating prior knowledge**)

To preview the text

- Read the heading on page 20. What does 'Protecting your patch' mean? (**previewing**)

 During reading

- Ask the children to read pages 20–30.
- As they read, ask them to think about how satellites are a type of defence for the planet.

 **After reading**

Returning to the text

- Ask the children
  - How do structures protect territory from attack and from water?
  - How do robins protect their territory?
  - How do satellites protect us?

Building fluency

- Listen to a clip from a radio naturalist programme on the BBC website. Note the presentational features. Encourage children to role-play being a naturalist broadcaster with pages from this book as the script.

> **Assessment point**
>
> Can the children create a radio broadcast using appropriate presentational features? AF2

Follow-up activities

Writing activities

- Children could write a descriptive account from their own experience of what it feels like to have a cold. (**short writing task**)
- Look at pages 14–15. Also, look at other examples of sales catalogues. Note the features: image, brief description, price. Make a catalogue of siege machines. (**short writing task**)
- Write a Martian report on defensive/attacking games such as football or netball. (**longer writing task**)

Other literacy activities

- Once the children have read all of the books in the cluster, orally review them and ask children to say which is their favourite and why. (**speaking and listening**)

> **Assessment point**
>
> Can the children justify their preferences using evidence from the books? AF4/5

Cross-curricular and thematic opportunities

- Research extinct animals. Find out how their defences failed. (**Science**)
- Use ICT to create an electronic catalogue of protective clothing used in skateboarding, biking and motor racing. (**ICT**)
- Research smoke alarms and design an advertising poster to persuade people to have one in their homes. (**PSHE, Art and design, DT**)